An Exercise In Catharsis

William M. McCleery

To order additional copies of this book, contact:
Xlibris
844-714-8691
www.Xlibris.com
Orders@Xlibris.com

ISBN: 978-1-6698-5774-7 (sc)
ISBN: 978-1-6698-5773-0 (e)

Print information available on the last page

Rev. date: 12/27/2022

If you are unhappy about your
life adding another person will
not change your opinion only
distract you

Lucky Numbers

11:11 4:44 3:33

An exersise in Catharsis

Dear reader

In these pages you will find letters, peoms, and thoughts I've
been having. I dont like proper poem structure, not because
I can't follow it but rather because rules have hindered my
creativity most of my life. If you relate to the passages you
have in hand I am so sorry life hasn't been kind to you, I take
pride in knowing I'm not alone in my struggles and I hope those
around you show you how much they love you.
Thank you for taking the time to read or even flip through my
mind. I found writting these pages helpful in understanding
my emotions. The hurt you feel is real, anyone who disregards
your outstretched hand when you need them most are not worthy
of you at your best. I have wasted far too much effort on
love that would never be ground benheath my feet when I was
drowning.
I am working on learning to love myself as much as I love
others. without limits and whole heartedly.

I hope you find comfort in my words, I hope you laugh, cry,
feel a bit of happieness when you close this book. I wish the
best for you in everything to come.

thankyou for taking the time to read my belly aching...
Yours

William (Matt) McCleery

This is a test for the new ribon in my RoyalCompanion
Black?
love? LUST?
            To what do I owe the pleasure this evening?
Cleerity? Not sobriety, no. Yet I see where I stand,

I stand atop a mountain I faught to the top of. But,
this is only the first peak.I will rise and fall, ever

climbing higher than my fall into depression. So long

is I remember in the valley the troubles from before,

sit with the emotion and allow myself to feel I can ov-

ercome all, so I swear...

William M McCleery

Now that I¡ve got that pretentiouse shit out of the way I am not
okay. I haven't been okay for a very long time. ᴍᴍᴍᴍᴍ But, I love
the potential ahead of me. I can feel that I'M on the right track.
something good will come of this and I am on the path to healing.
This is a very hard time in my life and I love all in my life.
Sorry I'm such an ass. I am healing, but there is so much left ahead
 I have internalised so much over the years. I'm surprised it took
this long for my colaps. It was bound to happen eventually.
I want to settle down one day in a cabin, spend my days tapping on
this old typewriter to the sound of a warm summer breeze through
spruce and oak trees. Fuck society, what has it ever for me, other
people are stressfull. Blow philosophical pot smoke at the spider
in the coroner. Coroner? who said anything about sending for the co-
oner, I'm not suicidal, mentally ill..yes...but I lack the vice to
 plundge blades intentially into my own skin. not intentially
 I prefer to pick and analyse my actions worry about all other outcomes

never the one infront of me. I destroy what I hold while wanting the
what if.
I need to live for what I have.
I love you all.

Matt

P.S.

Hold me accountable to the man I know I can be.

Dearest love,

How do I know that you are real? I have been lead astray so many times
I have faught for love that was never real. I have faught for
affection and affirmation from those indifferent to my health.
I am so tired, I am exhausted from the effort I put into unrecipro-
cated infatuation. Maybe, some loved me, Jenna, Madison I hurt them
both without knowing the extent of my actions. I hold myself accoun-
table for the pain I cause by chaseing unknown outcomes.

I am ashamed of what I have and continued to do for so many years.
You all deserved better. I tried to be the best partner I could be
without taking my own health into account. I have to be selfish now.

I have to be better if I ever hope to be happy. I have to be better
before I can feel the love I so crave. I am not ready to break another
heart just to feel some assemblance of happieness that fades faster
than the high of my chemical dependance. I am ready to feel, learn,
grow into the man I want to be.

THIS WILL HURT... But, it's time I experience

without supression, without hiding my emotions, my thin skin will

bleed as it should. I am the maker of my own undoing but also the creator of

my own sanity. I am on the right path but I have to heal before I

can take another step further towards my dreams.

Learn from my mistakes.

Your friend
Will M. McCleery

To fule a dream...

Tearing paper from binding,
Folding, creasing, and tearing again.
I fill my leaflet with earth
Folting over paper in my fingers,
the taste of ink
Psalm 13:2
"how long must I take counselin my soul,
and have sorrow in my heart all the day?"
Light, inhale, exhale,

The First Draft

My pen scratches across the page
inbossing the page with my thoughts, ink not flowing
the taste of ink, 959. EMERADD
scratching again across the page with ink, not mind
what was it?
the inspiration from before?
shit...

Thereïs something about a tattered page. The distinction
that something has made this page undesirable xxxxxx comp-
ared to the page under it. There's nothing wrong with it.
It is a piece of paper, perhaps some ink smudged, dirt from
under someones fingernails... more than likley your own.
Wasteful.
XXXXXXXWXXXXXXXXXXXXXXXXXXXXXXXXXXXXXXXXXXXXXXXXXXXXXX
XXXXXXXXXXXXXXXXXXXXXXXXXXXXXXXXXXXXXXXXXXXXXXXXXXXXXXXX

I love typeing. the mistakes and typos of which I know there
are many. But, this is free thought writing for me. I'm XX
talking to you, the reader whom whoever that may be.
Probably ony me.

William M. McCleery

SPIDER ON THE WALL

I'm sorry you had to watch this from your perch upon our
wall.
The fighting, the yelling, I doubt you understandthese words
but I still Feel guilty for making you watch.
I wass supposed to kill you weeks ago.
I couldn't bring myself to do it, the mosquitoes would feed
on me and you on them.
We had an understanding... just as she and I had an understanding

I still won't kill you now that she's left, I'm sorry you had
to watch this from your perch upon my Wall.

-William K. Killeen

Every fucking time

How &&& do you tell someone they've hurt you?
How can you if they don't even know how much you care?
How you hurt yourseIf, burning their words into your
    brain, minor acts of compassion, acts that made you
      fall. Not in love, no that's imposible... right?
        I hope so. I fall in love to easily, or have
    I ever truly been in love? Can I feel loved &&XXX
        by others? I think I meant it last time...
          no I'm sure I did. I remember her being
            nervous shuffling her feet with a stupid grin
              . We were in a hostel in paris. I meant it.
                Makes what happened so much worse. I'm
                sorry... means shit to you now.
                Someone new just did the same to me.
                    Ideserved it. I've been numbing
                      the past few days. I dont like
                        feeling how muchof a fucking
                        waste of space trash human
                          being I am. Sefl righteous
                            whore of a man.
        I haven't eaten yet today. I should
probably eat something, I
feel a bit sick. No, I want
      another coffee, I need to get somework done
                  . Distract yourself. you can process it later
                          you have deadlines to meet
              appearences to keep and all that

            bulshit selfcare upkeep nonsence.
                  when was the last time i
                    got out of bed before noon?
                      It's okay? I'm still
                      breathing,
              choking
          on
              s
              m
                o
                  ke

They say the first thing you forget is their voice.
So I try to remember yours every day.
I remember the last time we spoke.
I promised I'd be back soon, but I was in exams
I remember now it felt leaving that lecture hall
Having finished my last university exam
How proud I was that grad was just around the corner
And how I got you and Granda tickets.
I wanted you there more than my parents.
Nanny you never left the hospital
You never got to see me walk across the stage
I wasn't ready to see you in that hospital bed
I wasn't ready to make Granda cry.
I'm still not ready to say goodbye...

We miss you, I miss you.
I still talk about you like you just stepped away
out of sight to make yourself a cup of tea.
I know you're gone
But, can't I just pretend for a little longer
That one day instead of seeing you on that shelf
I'll hear your thick Glasgow accent ask if I'd like a cup.

SOMETIMES PEOPLE LEAVE US AND WE DON'T
                KNOW WHY

THE UNIVERSE IS NOT AGAINST YOU, APPARENTLY

IT'S OK TO CRY IF YOU HAVE TO, EVEN IF
                YOU DONT

I understand why things happened the way they did
But, with respect it hurt
So fuck yourself, I'm done.

I started smoking weed in highschool
I remember buying a single gram and stretching
it as long as I could
I smoked at least that just now
to forget your stupid smirk

Test
Test
Test

I understand why you used sex to numb yourself
I get it and I'm sorry your home life was so
hard you felt the need to escape in my arms
but you moved away for school
I went down on one knee
I was a fool

18=D (•.•) Y (•.•)

I dont know what day it is anymore

It's such a Chiche I'm ashamed of it. Not being able
to work without trauma fuling my writing and art. It's
idiotic to think what I'm capible of is only posible
impared but that logic only appears here, on this page.
My mind spirals away from logic as I repeat past trauma
still remembering the lessons from before. The more
you know about the past the more prepared you are for
the future. I used th think that only for world events
that politicians would restart old wars, fear and hate
vs knowledge and acceptance. WE teach tollerance but
to tollerate is merely to hate behind their back. Diff-
rences petween people should be accepted and celebrated
You are no differentxxxx than anyone else except you
are no one but yourself.

I dont know if the last passage makes a coherant thought
but it is the action in writin g the passage that proves
the point. I am me. I write, I am an Artist, and I am
human. I have made mistages that I must atone for.

                    I am Me

          and I am learning to live with myself.

An Exhistential Crisis and a hard place

Thats generally how I describe my life.
Blowing smoke and contemplating what it means to be me.
What it means to be me is like flying a plane
thats engine's stalled
nose down falling faster and faster
air flowing over the wings,
If I time this right the lift genorated will send me back
up into the sky.
I pull the throttle and try to lift the nose
One day I wont be able to pull this stunt anymore.
I8ll pull back on the stick and nothing will happen
but till then I'll enjoy this up and down routine
as best I can.

I'm soaring high but for how long.
I'm cutting the engine to save fule
I want to go farther than a single tank will take me
I want to know what it's like to fly without fear of falling

Dear Dad

My depression is not your fault. You are a good dad. I know
you always tried your best with me, wanting the best for me
in school and in scouting. I know you care. I hope you're
proud of the man I have become. I am a good friend, loved
but tourmented .
You said you never wanted me to be a child of divorce, but
how it's affected me was never in you're controle. I can't
look to you or mom for advice because you don't have a cule
more than I do.
Dad I remember when I was younger you used to yell at mom
I cant remember what for, but all my earliest memories are
of you yelling or being scared of being yelled at. I don't
understand why that is your responce to any form of conflict
when clearly I think you can see it doesn't work for you.
The world is a scary enough place as it is. why add to it?
Dad I am scared to lose you, the world isn't the same place
you grew up in anymore. It is still just as crule and unfor-
giving but the times of your hardships have changed.
The worlds just as fucked up now as it was then but now,
it's my genorations problems now. you need to take your
time, stop and breathe a little

CRAP CRAP CRAP CRAP CRAP CRAP CRAP CRAP CRAP CRAP CRAP CRAP
YOU CANT WRITE, YOUR DAD WAS WRITE, YOU CANT BE A WRITER
IF YOU CANT SPELL.

Sometimes I imagine full conversations with the people in
my life. Planning these interactions before they happen only
to have the actual event never go to plan. Sometimes I forget
what was a real interaction and what was just in my head.
When I can't tell normally nothing bad comes about, but I
have done this somany times that this stranger I barely know
puts a smile on my face... So I'm sorry I can be a bit much
I thought we were friends or more but it was just a daydream

My dreams are always better than my reality.

I told someone the other day that all I want is a bit of
mental stability in my life... might have been to honest
but I'm done lying that I'm okay. I just thought if you wanted
to actually know me I should be upfront with you.
Judging by your lack of responce that wasnt what you were
looking for... you did say *no hookups*

I have been in love three times.
I have said I love you to four people.
Of the times I meant it one of them was you.
I 'm sorry I couldnt say it in a way you
could ever believe me.

Jon's First time writting on my typewritter...

Me and matt and andrew went out for wings at coops.
It is 2020 we will be playing zombies tonight while listening
to flet-wood mac... Andrew is listening to matt hum while
reading matts previous writing piece.

My mom has just brought us down some cinnamon buns matt eats
one after having three pounds of wings for dinner earlier

This will be the end of my first piece but there may be another..

I'm still breathing

Sometimes I walk, I walk till I run out of ways to drown out
my thoughts, this constant hum in my ear of wasted potential

I run out of ways to ignore that it feels like I'm drowning

I'm not an addict; at least I wouldn't go that far yet. I can
walk XXXXX away for a while but sitting in this feeling always
brings me back.

To friends that know I give the option, honesty or a more com-
fortable answer.

I feel like I'm holding back a wave that only gets bigger every
day
or
I'm still breathing

It's not a lie, it hasn't killed me yetbut I'm tired of hiding
it. Of holding back the wave for someone else's convience...

Screams FUCK in a microphone for dramatic effect

If I could sing
I'd write punk songs
not sad poems about trauma

Every song would be for the revolution in my head

FUCK COPS
FUCK POLITICIANS
FUCK MY EX'S
and fuck you Mom

electric banjo rift

FUCK!

I dont have an EDIPUS complex

No it's okay you used me as a sex toy knowing I had feelings
for you

It's okay you don't want to date me because "I'm too healthy"
then sleep with me and walk out of the bedroom.

I just noticed you have vague similarities to my mother so
don't worry, I never want to touch you again anyway.

I like my days off, where I can sit and stare off...
I feel whats coming.

I wasn't productive today. I wasted a whole day stoned reapete-
ing old habits. I psychoanalyzed my past for a reason to write,
till the only words I wrote were self-deprocating faulsities
I hate myself most days for actions and events I fabrocated
excuses for. My mental health is not an excuse. I can't say
I'm crazy and get out of this Trial, unfortunatly I'm self
aware. I have lied to soften blows when the truth seemed too
painful. I tried to shealter you and XXXXXX so many from my
apathetic catastrophy of a life some would call a comedy.
Where the punchline is I'm running from happieness while wishing
for it...

Another self-care plan I'll abandon before it becomes
a habit:
        - Cook more often, try to only have take out afew
        days a week. You can cook better anyway.
        - Practice yoga sober
        - Write when you're on a high point, not just high
        on a low point.
        - Talk to your grandfather more often.
        - Apoligise again to your friends.

Remember what Nicole said "Self-care is productive." theres
nothing wrong with taking a day to yourself but you need
to vocalise that to others.

Don't punish yourself for things you didn't do.

Attachment styles

I function better in relationships
Just something constant
The stability keeps me grounded
But, not always happy

Happieness is realitive and not
Simply smiling

I can smile to hide a lot from you, I'm done
hiding how I feel from people. My deamons
ruin my attempts at closure. My fears stop
me from putting in any real effort...

I want to love and feel loved without conditions.
I dont want treatment passed off as a cure in a tiny
white bottle.
I want to be secure and healthy.
I am anxiouse to the point I overcompensate as
avoidant.

Men are TRASH
Afew words by a man on how men are skum.

A man will say he's terrified to have a daughter
because of how the world treats women. But, ignore
that his roommate raped a freshmen and heard her
calling for help.
Then in the morning make "I'm sorry" eye contact
instead of actually doing something.

Maybe not every man knows a rapist but every
man knows a victum.

I wish the story at the top of this page was
just an example and not something that happened
and was sweaped under the rug by their collage.

It's more thant teaching Consent
It's more than making boys Accountable

And if you can't help stop it
YOU'RE A PART OF IT...

Medicated

There's too many unknowns. Today I've
written four pieces. I took a shower, made
four cups of coffee, smoked four packed bowls
I had four exhistential crisis, four times
I put down my pen, and four times I picked it
up again.

I dont think I need to be medicated even
though I've spent the last four days in a void.

What if these were the last four I feel
the need to write, I never pick up a pen or
type a page. I want to feel not simply numb.
I already dissassociate so why should I use
an alternate.

Because, I'm scared... and thats okay. One
day I may be willing to try.

There lies the problem, it's always someday
never today...

Trope

My life is like a bad coming of age movie
where the mom has a terminal illness that
causes the family to crumbleand the child
acts out, or is such a people pleaser they're
too scared to leave and trauma can be fixed
with a hug.

    Except that$ nnot how trauma works so
I'm bitchin' and whining into the void
cracking jokes.

    A hug would be nice though if you find
the time.

Someone died today

I met them once, "call me Grandma".
Can't say more than that, their
life to be written by another...

But, the joy of their being shone
through.

I met'Grandma' to take her
photograph. Her triumph, on her terms,
was planned in two weeks time.

It's not a triumphto those who'd rather
hold your hand just an moment longer.

Someone died today...
Slipped off,meditating into a dream.
Undenyably better sounding than to leave
this world kicking and screaming;

So in life, as in death.
I know which one I'd rather, to what will
probably be an ironic end.

The end is always the same though...
Someone died today, and we all have to
deal with it in our own way... Poorly.

William M McCleod

It's funny when I realise I've been
disassociating I'm usually high getting
out of the shower. Seeing the state of
how I left my room. Then get distracted
by self-care.
But your hair up, eat oranges, take a
magnisium tablet. Questioning,when did
I eat last, why does my body hurt, coffee
or water.
It's funny when... what was the thought?

My selfworth is tied to my work, something
only I will experience because it's my
work. I abandon projects when I can see
the finished product. Stopping, procrastonat
will I finish the project or forever
be afraid to show myself.

Regergatated Therapy for Friends I needed
to hear myself:

I'm here if you want to talk.
I will listen, I may not always know
what to say but I promise you I will
listen.
Maybe repeat an aniquedote from my therapist
Offer a hug if yo u want one. A drink
if you feel you need one.

You need to hear what you're saying
just as much as you need to say it.

What might bring a sence of
fufillment:
- renting a studio space
- freelance writing
-getting back into street photo-
graphy
- spend more time reading
- work on "May is my Grandmother"
publication
    - look into self publishing
      as an art book
- apply to art shows
-cook more
- talk to jon and andrew more
often

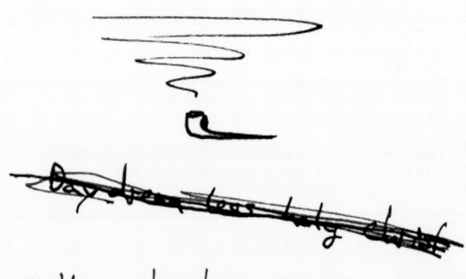

- Make shorter lists

Capitalism

I have come a long way from where I
was last year.
I should be proud of the work, the ground
I've covered to be where I am now.
Yet I still feel like I need to earn
my own happiness.
Like its some kind of prize to by chance
at birth, or slave your life away in
the hope of one day having a callosed
handful of happy memories.
I should be proud of the work I put in,
the ground covered; but I'm in a drivethru
Ordering :
- 24yr AngstyMeal
    * Trauma (side*)
- Rx Shake
    * EXTRA sprinkles
    * EXTRA whipped cream

Total:
Will to live.

Life's a McBitch

" I'm surprised you're an only child"

I remember vividly a teacher in school on the
first day dividing the class in her effort to
get to know the class. "Who has brown hair?"
my classmates and I stood oposite eachother.
"Who has pets at home?" a few left my side
"who has siblings?" and just like that I was
alone. "Matt your face, why's your face turning
red?"
"because everyone is staring at me" a ter that
I started to lie, saying my familywas bigger
than just the three of us. Was bigger that just
me hiding at the top of the stairs listening
to my parents fight my entire childhood.
People always have the same reaction expecting
me to be spoiled but that must be the steryotype
for a functioning family.
What it means to be an only child like me is
finding ways to put on a smile, practicing in
the mirror every morning. Faking one to tell
yourself you're fine because heaven forbid they
hear you cry and tell you to get over it.
I had no one to share with so you assume I'm
selfish. I had no one to share with so I'd give
everything to anyone willing to break that lonleynes
From compulsive lieing to unburdoned honesty
I'm scared I'll always be the child alone at
the top of the stairs, but at what cost?
I carried thoes habits into relationships hoping
I was finally safe only to learn I'd keep myself
alone...

Dear Mom and Dad

We don't talk about things... which is strange and hard.
We were a family at least at some point I think and as an
adult I find myself looking for any stability to hold
onto. I don't blame either of you for anything, I am
the product of my environment. I just wish we were there
for eachother more.
Mom you have been fighting breast cancer for so long.
I know you're scared but you cannot use it to blackmail
me into doing what you want, cannot use it as a means
to justify your actions. I remember sitting on the couch
in XXXXXX Omy's living room, you told Aunt Erica and
my cousins saying "Matthew's the only one that doesn't
know now ". You were standing behind me! Do you think
I'm deaf or dumb? Whenever you bring up your health and
don't lie or tell half-truths I'm fed a story that you
were scared. I was scared I'd lose my Mom! Howdare you
blackmail me with your health. If that offends you, I'M
right and you won't change. I have been angry with you
for so long because it feels like you forced yourself
to go through this alone. Heaven forbid you forgive
someone insead of holding a grudge ruining the relationship.
I hated Dad for most of my life because of you, instead
of comforting me you panic and place blame, you dont
comunicate how you feel except under your breath.
I learned to treat people like this from you and I feel
empty. The tools you need are infront of you but you refuse
to teach yourself. Digging a grave when you could be planting
a garden.
When you divorced Dad I was an Adult under the law, look*
ing back I was still just a child stunted dealing with
the trials and trauma I remember in fragments of my
childhood. I clung to Nanny and Granda like a ra it
at sea. They were solid and stable, I could build my
life around them.

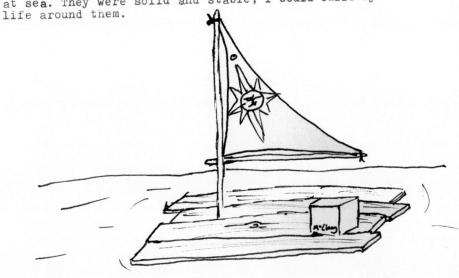

I woke up everyday scared Granda would wake up alone.
Now that he does I'm scared I'll lose him too. He watched
me grow into the man I am today. Neither of you know
me, I'm to blame for that. But, why would I opan up to
immediate critism. I don't think you'd get me, I'm a ne-
rvous wreck most of the time. Smoke weed to treat my
ADHD and Depression, while drinking enough coffee to
feel tremors putting my anxiety to work on something
I meant to do a week ago. I am the worst parts of both
of you. I am ambitious and would die for people who'd
never lift a finger to help me and thats been a problem
my whole life, I am the problem solver in every situation
because as a child I tried to fix your merrage.
That never should have been my responcibility.

I envy people who are close to their parents, people
who can tell the truth about how they feel to those they
love... because I am in constant pain...
      Nanny is gone and I lost my liferaft. I'm not ready
to lose Granda too. I know so little about him, I want
to know how he met Nanny. I want to know if the shy opened
up and he just knew because so far everytime I tell a
woman I love them I ruin it and again I'm sinking...
              ... lost at sea.
I want to know what the ground beneath my feet feels
like. I'm learning not to tie my happieness onto other
people and learn to live wIXHHYXAXX with myself.

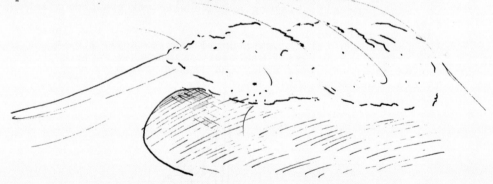

I'm proud of who Ive become all things considered, I
know I am on the right path for the first time in my
life and I am excited for the future. But, I'm scared
because everything is changing so fast. We're free fa-
lling together, we won't land together. Everything I
have ever known as our family has been an open hound
but it was still family. I'm losing that instead of healing,
not that I'd know where to start...

Dad, you're so angry and I've never understood why.
you need to stop picking fights. I remember when I was
a kid hiding in the basement listening to the two of
you fight. "Alright, Trevor alright" "No! It's not alr*
ight!" ... I would have just left in your shoes,
despite the trauma I appreciate you sticking around.
I understand a lot of what you feel. I feel it too, but
you need to breathe. I am a result of my environment.

        It is so hard to write this because of all
the emotions I feel for both of you. I have imagined
having you read this hundreds of times. everytime hoping
It won't start a fight, imagining what closure might
feel like... I imagune it feels good. I wake up from
these daydreams feeling hollow,throwing work and XXXX
pot smoke at the issue. Filling it like an air balloon
anxious about the fall. Ever blowing smoke at the prob-
lem soaring higher.
Dad I always doubt myself because your rule#q is that
you're always right. You're a smart man but most of the
time you're wrong. I tell people I don't like being told
I cant do something, that I'll XXXXXX prove them wrong.
You gave me a spiteful workeffort, and self-doubting
workethic. I am never right XXX always wrong.
The first time I tried to talk to a doctor about my me-
ntal health they laughed saying what i was feeling wass
a result of a sinus infection. I didn't believe them
but I'm still hoping I'm a hypochondriac, this is all
a figment of my imagination ... wake up wiping sleep
from my eyes like it never happened... only everything
did happen, is happening, and will keep happening if
I dont write this.
Un interupted crying into the void with my typewriter.

        I'm trying to see you both as people, not
just my parents, not just a void in my life.

I know this was ~~difint~~ hard to read
I don't know if either of you will understand
what I'm saying but I love you both
and I'm healing slowly
        _ Matthew

Can I write?

yes

I can

Putting in the work...

How much pain does it take to walk away from those who
cause it?
When every time you act on advice from liscenced therapists
drugs, hallucinogenics, tarot card readings, to open up
more people dismiss your trauma because they; They turned
out fine.
I have been told how to be happy on the same breath they
told me I'm fine.
How much time does it taketo heal?
Because, I'm tired of getting advice on how to put in the
work, when I'm putting in the fucking work.

"no need to be so sensitive, you need thicker skin"

I'll admit small things can set me off. I am done hiding
my emotions.
How am I a bleeding heart if its been festering for
so long...

BUY IN BULK

Life is fucking hard for everyone
You'll probably have to share

Roll one so that it's fair
Two times around the room

Grey like a tomb

Sonder: to think that everyone
has a story not so diffrent than
yours that shaped them into the
person they are.
pain, love, happieness,
sadness

Sonder... better make it an ounce
this time

Life seems like a Lie disguised as Truth.

Where truth, actual Truth is hidden because we choose to ignore what's infront of us.

Lofty statements about the human condition.

The truth that I found is that I cause my own problems.
Passing blame for my actions is harmful to myself.

Bridget, fuck off

For years I called you crazy while I did the same thing.
I caught myself medicating with intamacy, treating my
depression with endorphins, numbing headaches with sex.
Finding validation from strangers saying I dont need to
change when now clearly I am the problem.
When you reached out, yes I was hostile, yes I was angry
Why? Because, you never knew the pain you caused me or
even considered I deserve an apoligie before trying to
enter my life again.

Do you even know you were in the wrong? Burning bridges
while still standing on them. I didn't.

So with respect I understand what you went through but
for the sake of wanting to be better than the person I
became after you or always was, stay out of my life.

You don't get to say you miss me.
I miss thinking the people I choose to be in my life
say they love me and mean it without a second thought.
You didn't cause my mental illnesses but tha t doesn't
give you the right to walk all over people.
Alexa was your friend yet you chose to harrass her
because you were bored, hiding behind a screen.
There are conciquences to your actions.

I regret meeting you most of the time because I wasted
the only secure relationship I've been able to have on
you and Madison deserved so much more than the pain I
caused. I should have given her the world compared to you.

I'M not writting this because I want a responce, or to
ever hear your voice. I'm writting this because I'm tired
I'm done having a ~~XXXXXX~~ memory of love that was never
real. This chapter of my life is doneand I'm leaving the
pain behind.

You dont have power over me anymore ~~so fuck off and go
to therapy.~~

VISIONS FROM MY FIRST ACID TRIP

WE WERE STANDING WAIST DEEP IN THE
WATER WITH THE SUN BEATING DOWN.
THERE'S NO KALEIDOSCOPE BUT WE JUST
WATCHED THE CLOUDS OVER HEAD, THE
TARMAGONS FLYING OVER THE WATER IN
A SINGLE LINE THAT SEEMED TO GO ON
FOREVER. WE STAYED THERE TILL SUNSET

I WAS ABLE TO TALK MYSELF OUT OF
THE VISIONS BECAUSE YOU WERE THERE

I can still see them like a dream
the vision of my parents hugging me
as a child. Telling them how I know
they never meant to hurt me, standing
there crying. In a second changing
wwe all aged older than we are now
their hair turning white as mine
thinned.
I should have told them years ago
and even now I put it off...

Neverending Critique

I hate how I stop myself from
liking things. That I judge
myself for enjoying anything
"It's pretentio use"
so what?
I wouldn't listen to a critic
if I already enjoyed the work.
so why am I listening to this
critic who's insessive jabbering
is perticularily why I dislike the
opinion in the first place.

I love taking mushrooms and
listening to jazz

Why should I stand in the
way of my own enjoyment

An Ode to Art School

"We'll teach you how to get paid to do what you love"
        The poster sat across from me as I rode the
subway to the same job I've had since graduation, the
same job that paid my touition. Touition that lined
other peoples pockets as I sew deeper ones with debt.
The colour pallet was dull and muted.
The Alumni (so I assume) smiled as tho they knew of
the lie being told with their identity. That somehow
their sucess could be tied to an institution. I wish
i could have attended in the days my old professors
studied, the days of five hundred dollas touition,
When you could take as many classes as you wanted so
Long as you left an hour for lunch. When they valued
less the art you were able to creat upon walking in the
Door and more what they could actually teach you.
My art school gained university status... so hurray
I have a Degree instead of a Diploma as if the diffrence
truly matters.
I miss the days when my sleep was deprived by the need
to creat something on top of the fourty hour work load
of all the essays about what I was creating to justify
it's existance. That it wasn't plagerized, I made something
with my own hands, of free thought, but not of Free will.
I was making something for the grades not the expressed
joy from my practice. Art is subjective. If my profe-
ssors didn't understand my premmis the critique would
save the grade. validation from my peers who understood
the workload, and then the grade would be bell curved.

I miss my peers who could see me. I miss my peers who
I'd spend hours with in the darkroom listening to eachothers
music as the Photographs slowly appeared in the developer
like magic.
Art school taught me that what I love is to creat with
my hands, the tactile nature of building on my emotions.
Creating ideas. Plato says art is a lie because it
is a representation of a representation. that only the
Idea is perfect. to which I reply, Nothing is perfect
not even the lie. I squabble enough with my own exhistance
to justify my need to make something as truth.
"Ii did not love them because they were perfect"
Beauty is in the deatail of the imperfections.

What I learned is that unless I am able to produce
I a m worthless. What I produce doesn't have to be
good or bad, meerly exhist. Why? Fuck it, Why not?
I wanted to make something, anything because for onec
people were paying attention to it. Spending time in
awe that this thing infront of them was so real and
beautiful. If my art was a mirror we'd call the viewer
Vail as if self love was a crime. It's exactly what we
need isn't it ? ...

A little more love for ourselves. Just exhisting. no
No purpose, what pourpose? I was born and now I'm here.
So was my art. Why should I tourment myself looking
for pourpose in what I do when the pourpose of what
I do was to fill the time of my exhistance... What meaningg
Art school filled the pourpose that was "just to be"
with "to make money doing it" as if money where a cure
to ailments I didn't know I had. I was already only
acutly aware of how poor I was before going to art school.
Sarcasm doesnt come across in text.
I remember drinking with a STEM student their name,
meaningless, the conversation meaningless, but they
were under the assumption because I chose to study art
I was dumb. So I turned the conversation to Philosophy
then politics, Environmental science,,trying to explain
that my education wasnt simlpy Art.
An expressive handjesture with a lit cigarrette...
The institution was a buesness selling dreams at the
cost of them. spitting out burnout artists at the cost
of fourty thousand dollars if you're a domestic artist.
Capitalism says tripple that for forigners because
"we take care of our own". I have a degree in what I
like to see as human value. Tho it doesn't matter.
How can it?
It's a piece of paper.
A promis that has been shoved down my throat since I
could open my eyes hoping to merely survive.
That Education and Schooling are the same when $ is
heald on high like God.
Now over educated I Critique the admissions poster
catching it in it's lies. wanting to take out a marker
to write "dont listen to their lies"
"make your art"
"I cant wipe my ass with my degree"
Art school created me... my parents slaved away their
lives to pay for my path to a better future when there
was never any promisland to begin with...
So I sit with the poster riding the subway. looking
at eachother with hollow expressions. An interview in
my head. Am I crazy... no I wouldn't be asking the question
if I actually was.
I'm an Artist with imposter syndrome... mistakes are
part of the process, the visible ones meake the work
great because you can see the flaws and love despite them.
Cleché and full of tropes because everything has been done.
That doesn't take away from what is and what is not.
duality. plurall exhistance .
IXXXXXXXXXXXXXXXXXXXXXXXXXXXXXXXXXXXXXXXXXXXXXXXXXXXXXXXXXXX

Sex, whisky, and poor decisions

A moment of extacy
A moment of bliss in the arms of a stranger but
for Only a moment,
A fleeting moment and once again
I find myself thinking of you.

Hold Tightly

Memories, Memories of those loved, lost,
Slipping between fingers and patterns.

Hold tightly to memories
Hold tightly to daydreams,
Fantasies, fallacies, tears, pain.

Breathe, feel, fall to pieces
Hold tightly to those who's eyes flicker
In your lives light.

Hold tightly to lessons learned
Beaten, bloodied, angry, breathe again.
Hold tightly to your attention.

Hold tightly as if your life
Were slipping through open hands
Hold tightly to your own forgiveness.

The pen in your hand writes the past.
Hold tightly to your presence,
Your peace, palpable pleasure XXX in
Perserverance.

Hold tightly,time is fleeting
Ever flowing through open hands
Moments and memories like sweet
Melodies.

Self Love Prenupt

I Promise to be mindful of my thoughts,
Emotions, and actions.
To do my best, the very best of XXXX
My ability to show myself extra Love and
Kindness in my life to come.
Forgive myself for the mistakes and patterns
Of my past.XXXXXXXXXXXXXXXX
I give myself permission to love myself completely.
I know the process will be lenghhy.
The journey full of valleys and mountains,
A metephorical landscape of sorrow,
With the promise land always just around the corner.

Loving myself, yourself doesn't need permission.
It doesn't need a companion...
              The journey never ends ...
          Find health and happieness in
          It's pursuit

Ground Glass

I wish more could view the world as I
have.
A watchful eye for moments endowed
with life.
Watching the passage of time on
ground glass.

Out an Introduction

Melancholy is madness in ones Monarch mind. Miserable
Meracahously with a metropolis at their doorstep.
Your therapist theroises tennitivly, Townsfolk to be
but a twinkling light upon your heart. Never to be
worthy of such a love because of the vocation I choose
and the location of my birth outside my control.
That the soul that stole your heart could never hold it.
How am I unworthy because of the location of my youth.
A maelstrom of memories. Stories we sew together into
identity, we are not where we happened to fall into
exhistance but the exhistance that falls into being.

Location is Happenstance.

When I die, turn my body to
dust and give me back to my
loved ones... finally I'll be able
to be with you all, though I
wish it was in life

stone against a
black sky...

ing for myself written
upon it.

D MY BEST

Printed in the United States
by Baker & Taylor Publisher Services